Margaret Walker with family and friends, 1992

MARGARET WALKER'S

'For My People'

A TRIBUTE

Photographs by Roland L. Freeman

University Press of Mississippi   Jackson and London

95 94 93 92   4 3 2 1

The paper in this book meets the
guidelines for permanence and dur-
ability of the Committee on Pro-
duction Guidelines for Book
Longevity of the Council on
Library Resources.

This book commemorates the fiftieth anniversary of the publication
of *For My People* by Margaret
Walker. It is published in conjunc-
tion with a special observance of
this anniversary and exhibit of
Roland Freeman's photographs at
Jackson State University in October,
1992, sponsored by the Margaret
Walker Alexander National Research
Center for the Study of the Twentieth Century African-American.

The public program at Jackson
State University and the publication
of this book have been made pos-
sible by the generous support of the
Mississippi Humanities Council, the
National Endowment for the
Humanities, and Trustmark National
Bank, Jackson, Mississippi. The
University Press of Mississippi and
Jackson State University gratefully
acknowledge the assistance of MHC.

The photograph on page one shows
Amy Garland and her mother,
Carolyn Farrow-Garland,
Washington, D.C., 1977.

In the photograph on page two
Margaret Walker Alexander gives a
special poetry reading to her grand-
children, neighbors, and students
from Jackson State University where
she taught for many years. Jackson,
Mississippi, 1992. Clockwise: seated
left, Myleme Ojinga Harrison;
Omoni Malik Hunt; Melanie Krisina
Williams; Karmisha M. Miller;
Jamian Sol Alexander; Tammiko
LaShawn Walker; Alferdteen Har-
rison; Sigismund W. Alexander;
Jarrett J. Williams; Monroe Adams
Johnson; center, Margaret Walker
Alexander, and her granddaughter,
Gwendolyn Gayle Williams.

Library of Congress Cataloging-in-
Publication Data

Margaret Walker's "For my people"/
    a tribute/photographs by Roland
    L. Freeman.
        p. cm.
        ISBN 0-87805-613-0
        1. Walker, Margaret, 1915- . For
    my people. 2. Afro-Americans in
    literature. I. Walker, Margaret,
    1915- . II. Freeman, Roland L.,
    1936-
    PS3545.A517F636 1992   92-28492
    811'. 52--dc20   CIP

*British Library Cataloging-in-Publication
data available*

FOR MY PEOPLE

For my people everywhere singing their slave songs repeatedly: their dirges and their ditties
and their blues and jubilees, praying their prayers nightly to an unknown god, bending their
knees humbly to an unseen power;

For my people lending their strength to the years, to the gone years and the now years and the
maybe years, washing ironing cooking scrubbing sewing mending hoeing plowing digging
planting pruning patching dragging along never gaining never reaping never knowing and
never understanding;

For my playmates in the clay and dust and sand of Alabama backyards playing baptizing and
preaching and doctor and jail and soldier and school and mama and cooking and playhouse
and concert and store and hair and Miss Choomby and company;

For the cramped bewildered years we went to school to learn to know the reasons why and
the answers to and the people who and the places where and the days when, in memory of
the bitter hours when we discovered we were black and poor and small and different and
nobody cared and nobody wondered and nobody understood;

For the boys and girls who grew in spite of these things to be man and woman, to laugh
and dance and sing and play and drink their wine and religion and success, to marry their
playmates and bear children and then die of consumption and anemia and lynching;

For my people thronging 47th Street in Chicago and Lenox Avenue in New York and Rampart
Street in New Orleans, lost disinherited dispossessed and happy people filling the cabarets
and taverns and other people's pockets needing bread and shoes and milk and land and
money and something—something all our own;

For my people walking blindly spreading joy, losing time being lazy, sleeping when hungry,
shouting when burdened, drinking when hopeless, tied and shackled and tangled among
ourselves by the unseen creatures who tower over us omnisciently and laugh;

For my people blundering and groping and floundering in the dark of churches and schools
and clubs and societies, associations and councils and committees and conventions, distressed
and disturbed and deceived and devoured by money-hungry glory-craving leeches, preyed on
by facile force of state and fad and novelty, by false prophet and holy believer;

For my people standing staring trying to fashion a better way from confusion, from hypocrisy
and misunderstanding, trying to fashion a world that will hold all the people, all the faces, all
the adams and eves and their countless generations;

Let a new earth rise. Let another world be born. Let a bloody peace be written in the sky. Let
a second generation full of courage issue forth; let a people loving freedom come to growth.
Let a beauty full of healing and strength of final clenching be the pulsing in our spirits and
our blood. Let the martial songs be written, let the dirges disappear. Let a race of men now
rise and take control.

The publication in 1942 of Margaret Walker's first book, *For My People,* thrust into national prominence the twenty-seven-year-old poet and her powerful words. In his foreword to that book, which won the 1942 Yale Series Younger Poets Award, Stephen Vincent Benet wrote that her poems "are full of the rain and the sun that fall upon the faces and shoulders of her people, full of the bitter questioning and the answers not yet found, the pride and the disillusion and the reality . . . She has spoken of her people so that all may listen."

Since publication of this book, few writers have communicated the essence of the African American experience as Margaret Walker has. "For My People," the title poem and probably the most well-known one in the collection of twenty-six, exemplifies Walker's special genius for capturing her people's spirit, rhythm, and meaning.

I came to know the power of Margaret Walker's poetry while a graduate student at the University of Kansas between 1967 and 1971. During those days African American lecturers, student leaders, and activists across the political spectrum recited "For My People" to identify the people for whom and of whom they spoke. It was not unusual to hear a moderate civil rights advocate and a less moderate civil rights advocate on the same platform use different verses of the poem to make their particular

point. I remember ending my remarks during a public meeting with these words from the last stanza of the poem: "Let another world be born . . . Let a second generation full of courage issue forth." The next speaker began his introduction of the Muslim minister by asking, "Why did she leave out the words 'Let a bloody peace be written in the sky'?" He then spontaneously recited the entire poem to justify African Americans' use of any means necessary to obtain justice and equality in America.

During my first visit to Jackson State University in 1970 I was virtually speechless in Walker's presence. Leonard Harrison, a professed revolutionary, who took me to the Black Studies Institute that Alexander was conducting, did most of the talking. I was fascinated to see an African American woman/intellectual express her opinions and cite sources for her points of view so well. I think back upon that meeting, and I believe it was the first time I had seen an African American female college teacher in action in the classroom. Since I had been the founding coordinator of the African Studies Program at the University of Kansas, my interests and Walker's were similar. Later, when I came to Jackson State University in the fall of 1972, I participated in all of the programs that Walker sponsored.

My admiration for Walker has increased as I have learned to know

her as a friend, scholar, writer, and wife and mother. Known in the academic community by her married name, Margaret Walker Alexander, Dr. Alexander is a model of excellence for the faculty and students at Jackson State University.

Through her lectures, her essays, and books Margaret Walker is widely known throughout this country. Her published works establish her as a major force in American literature of the twentieth century. In addition to *For My People,* her books include *Jubilee* (1966), winner of a Houghton Mifflin Fellowship Award and an international best seller. She has also published *Prophets for a New Day* (1970), *October Journey* (1973), *Poetic Equation: Conversations with Nikki Giovanni and Margaret Walker* (1974), *For Farish Street Green* (1986), *Richard Wright: Daemonic Genius* (1988), *This is My Century: New and Collected Poems by Margaret Walker* (1989), and *How I Wrote Jubilee and Other Essays on Life and Literature* (1990).

The inspiration for this photographic tribute to Margaret Walker on the fiftieth anniversary of her publishing career came during one of Roland Freeman's early morning telephone calls when I mentioned plans for a celebration in October of 1992. He immediately indicated that he was interested in curating a commemorative photographic exhibit with a publication for the occasion. He then called Margaret

Walker, who was excited about the idea. Conversations with the University Press of Mississippi indicated a similar enthusiasm. As director of the Margaret Walker Alexander National Research Center, I was thrilled and planned to coordinate the project.

Over the last seventeen years Roland Freeman's skills as a documentary photographer and my skills as an oral historian have cemented a friendship. We have contributed to each other's projects, shared common friends, participated together on many programs, and communicated frequently. As Roland and I talked that February morning, my familiarity with his work, work habits and professional standards all told me that the project Roland had in mind would be the centerpiece of this commemorative celebration. Equally as important was the fact that Freeman's life work exemplifies the goal of the Margaret Walker Alexander National Research Center, which focuses on documenting, preserving, and interpreting the life of the twentieth century African American.

Freeman, who lives in Washington, D.C., is a free-lance photographer, editorial magazine photographer, collector of black folk art, documentary photographer, teacher and lecturer, and director of the Group for Cultural Documentation. Freeman's project "While There Is Still Time," has been documenting black culture throughout the African Diaspora. As a Smithsonian Institution Office of Folklife Program photographer in folklore since 1972, his work has been exhibited throughout the United States, Europe, and Africa. His publications are *Something To Keep You Warm: The Roland Freeman Collection of Black American Quilts from the Mississippi Heartland* (Mississippi Department of Archives and History, 1979), *Southern Roads/City Pavements: Photographs of Black Americans* (International Center of Photography, 1982, accompanying an international touring exhibit), *Stand By Me: African American Expressive Culture in Philadelphia* (Smithsonian Institution's Office of Folklife Programs, 1989), and *The Arabbers of Baltimore* (Tidewater Publishers, 1989).

As Margaret Walker Alexander exemplifies the highest standards of literary artist and scholar, Roland Freeman exemplifies the highest standards of a documentary photographer. The photographs in this book interpret Margaret Walker's fifty-year achievement in a manner that stimulates the imagination of all ages in the American public.

This volume fits within a distinguished tradition of poet and photographer collaborations. Significant examples are *Sweet Flypaper of Life* by Langston Hughes, with photographs by Roy De Carava; *In Our Terribleness* by Amiri Baraka, with photographs by Billy Abernathy; and *The Harlem Book of the Dead* by James Van DerZee, Owen Dobson, and Camille Billops. Yet the publishing relationship of Walker and Freeman, reflected in the present book, stands out as the first time a photographer has published a photographic essay as a tribute to the poet.

This book is a tribute to Margaret Walker Alexander, a twentieth century American who has forcefully and movingly revealed the essence of her people, their struggles, their rhythms, their celebrations, and their magic. Freeman is of the "generation full of courage" coming forth and taking control that Margaret writes about in the closing lines of her signature poem, "For My People."

Let a second generation full of courage issue forth; let a people loving freedom come to growth. Let a beauty full of healing and a strength of final clenching be the pulsing in our spirits and our blood. Let the martial songs be written, let the dirges disappear. Let a race of men now rise and take control.

We thank you, Roland, for your talent and your courage. And we thank you, Margaret, for inspiring and empowering all who know you and hear the beauty and power of your words.

Alferdteen Harrison, Director
Margaret Walker Alexander Research Center, Jackson State University

LOOKING BACK

A Conversation with Margaret Walker

What do you think is the importance of Roland Freeman's photographic tribute to you on the fiftieth anniversary of your first publication?

This is the first time that I can recall any illustration or depiction in photographs of what I was saying in the poem. I have always depended on the energies of the poem itself to communicate to people what I was thinking. Now after fifty years, this is a wonderful tribute to the book *For My People,* covering not only the title poem but the twenty-six or more poems in the book as a whole. This is something different, and I hope that it will help to remind many people of what my commitment has been to my own people throughout these fifty years.

Roland Freeman has done the same thing with his photographs that many black writers have tried to do with their poetry or their stories. He has gone through the South and shown the life of our people in all areas, and this has been not just from the standpoint of race, but of class: poor people, working people, people whose opportunities have been limited and who have struggled on for some kind of existence. That is what his photographs represent.

I am very proud and pleased

This interview was conducted by Alferdteen Harrison on 8 May, 1992, at the home of Margaret Walker.

and honored to have Roland Freeman do this book. I think it will be a further step toward popularizing the poetry. People generally don't like poetry, but everywhere I have gone and read my poetry people have liked it, and I think these pictures will enhance its popularity. I am grateful to Roland because I think he has the right concept—he understands the social significance of what I try to say. And therefore it pleases me very much.

So, to have this photographic tribute fifty years after you wrote your first piece is—very appropriate.

What strikes me is that I wrote these poems for the most part in the decade of the 1930s. It was a period of depression—economic depression—and black people suffered along with everyone else from lack of jobs, from lack of standard housing, from lack of appropriate schooling. We were literally outcast from the general society. But then there were poor white people, too, and poor working people. It was a time when the unions were struggling to have collective bargaining, to have a forty-hour week, and all these entered into the picture of economic depression. A number of my poems indicate that. In fact, all through my poetry, from the thirties through the eighties, you will find concern for poor black people.

So this is a really fitting kind of collaboration, tied together in the nineties?

I think so. I think it is a kind of document that gives a picture of fifty years of struggle. And I have some poems in the book, that first book, talking about our struggle, about our problems, economic problems more than political, but seeing them as basic to the problems of racism. I think that Roland's pictures go along with the poems: they are companion pieces. And I find in them certain subjects that are clearly the subjects of the poems. For example, Roland's photographs say a great deal about the family, and I have poems that call attention to members of the family. Not just the children or the parents or the grandparents, but the extended family—that has always been one of the subjects in my poetry.

I'd like you to reflect back to the circumstances of publishing this work. How did you choose a publisher? How did you come to publish this book?

This is a nice and interesting story. I was a student at Northwestern University when I first heard of the Yale Younger Poets competition. I knew the reputation of Yale University, and I knew something about university presses. I have now had three books published by university presses. For me they stand for a kind of quality, not necessarily true with all commercial publishers, and frequently the university press is not interested in making money as such, but in finding the quality of life that I especially wanted to express in my poetry.

I entered the Yale Younger Poets competition five years before I received the award. The first time I sent my manuscript of poetry away, I must have been twenty or twenty-one years old, and that was before I wrote the poem "For My People." The manuscript came back as fast as I sent it, and I realized that it didn't get any further than the press before they turned it around and sent it back. In 1939 I was studying at the University of Iowa, and I discovered that a number of people who had been at the university in the writer's workshop had entered that contest and some had won. I didn't know at the time that my teacher, Paul Engle, had won that award ten years before I did. But I decided on my own to send my manuscript again. In January of 1940 I again sent my manuscript to Yale, but this time I wrote a cover letter to the editor, who was Stephen Vincent Benet, and I sent the manuscript and the letter directly to him. For the first time the publishers there did not send it back without his seeing it. It was his personal mail, and he got a chance to read it for the first time. Almost six months passed before I heard from him, and then he wrote a very encouraging letter, saying he regretted that I did not win the prize but that he was very impressed with my work and hoped that, if I had not published it in another year, I would send it back. I graduated from Iowa with a master's degree

that summer, and the next year I sent my manuscript back, in 1941. That was the third or fourth time I think I had sent it. And he wrote again another apologetic letter but pointing out that my work was valuable and that I mustn't be discouraged: it would eventually be published.

The next year—1942, the year I won—I did not even submit my manuscript. I was convinced, as Richard Wright has said, that Yale wasn't going to publish any black writer. So I didn't send it. I was surprised to hear a colleague tell me at a college language meeting that Stephen Benet had said I was going to win the prize that year. I was surprised because I had not even submitted my manuscript. But when I went back to work, I received a telegram asking me to send it to him at his summer address, if I was still eligible, and also to wire him in New York that I had done so. And that is the way I got it published.

That's a beautiful story. How did that make you feel?

I think that I must have known, as young as I was, that to publish with a very prestigious publisher would not only add luster to my work, it would give me a chance to be better known. I was in my twenties, and fifty years later I realize that was the auspicious beginning of my career. For a long time after that I didn't publish any poetry, and people assumed I was a one-book poet. But my teacher at Northwestern told me I didn't have to rush out and publish again right away, that the book would last the

rest of my life, and if I didn't do anything for the next fifteen to twenty years, it would be time enough. That was precisely what I did.

So, how did you arrive at that title, "For My People"?

It is the title of one of the poems—the title poem—most of which I have often said I wrote in fifteen minutes on a typewriter. I think it was just after my twenty-second birthday and I felt it was my whole life gushing out—as I had felt about my people all my life. "For My People" was just the way I started the poem. It was what I wanted to say, it was that and nothing else. But at the end of six or seven stanzas I didn't know how to finish it. I kept wondering what the conclusion should be. Nelson Algren was on the writer's project in Chicago, and I let him read the poem. And he asked me, "What do you want for your people?" And that gave me the answer, and the last stanza. Even fifty years later I am satisfied that what I said then is what I still want now.

Did the publishers want to change the title?

I have been very fortunate with the books that I have written. I know that often publishers change titles, but nobody talked about changing the title of that book. It was the title of my thesis for the masters degree. When *Jubilee* came along, the publishers wanted to change that name. I held fast to *Jubilee,* and when the sales conferences took place they asked the salesmen if they didn't think we should change the title, because should change the title, because they had researched and found about a half dozen—six or seven— other books with the title *Jubilee.* But the salesman told them no, they could sell that book with the title *Jubilee,* and the publishers had to abide by that. I have never had a book with the title completely changed. It is always what I choose. I know that doesn't happen with many people. I happen to know Richard Wright's books were not named by him, that publishers typically named them because he did not have a name for them. but I always had my own titles and I won't let anyone change them.

What are some of the highlights, or pivotal events, that have either affected your career or that are significant about black life since your first publication?

I have had a very great struggle over the fifty years to try to be a writer, as well as teacher, and a wife, and a mother, and to go on lecture tours, and it has been a struggle in more ways than one— largely financial. But I was determined to do certain things and I took chances. Unfortunately, I pushed myself always too hard and I was always ill as a result of it. But I was fortunate in winning prizes. For the ten books I have written, I have received at least ten prizes. The first was from the Rosenwald Foundation for the book *For My People,* and then I received two Ford Foundation grants, one for *Jubilee* and one for the Richard Wright book. I have received money from the National Endowment for the humanities, a senior fellowship to do research on the Richard Wright

book, and I discovered that the wonderful Lyndhurst prize I received four or five years ago was given to me because of the Richard Wright book. Every book has been financed by another book, and cash prizes are not always the usual thing. I have had a lot of honors, but the cash prizes have financed my creative work. I couldn't have done it on my teacher's salary, and I had nobody to serve as a patron, but government and foundation sources paid for my creative career. *I think that is an excellent statement for your career of fifty years. The final area we want to pursue is what do you see, other than this illustrious career, that has been generated as a result of For My People?*

I think that there are two ways to measure the success of a book. The general public wants to know right away how much money you made. That has always been a joke because ordinarily books just don't make a lot of money. My books have sold well, however. *For My People* went through eight printings before it went out of print, and when the University of Georgia collected my poems and reprinted them, that meant the ninth printing of *For My People.* Even though it might not have sold for much at first, it started out at two dollars and a half and later sold for five dollars. I discovered a printed edition that sold for eight dollars, and people have told me they have gone in old bookstores and found copies selling for as much as thirty-five dollars—not coming to me of course. But I think for a writer's first book of poetry to have sold

nine printings is very good indeed. It doesn't happen all the time.

For My People got off to a very illustrious start. Winning the Yale Award for Younger Poets was a distinction in itself. And when I went to New York to promote the book, I was invited to the *New York Herald Tribune* Book and Author luncheon at the hotel Astor where I read my poetry. That began my career as a lecturer. Everywhere I went and people heard me read my poetry, the word spread to others that I could read my poetry well. I have never lacked for engagements; I simply couldn't always fill them.

Jubilee has been a tremendous success. I understand three million copies have been printed and the publishers admit that they have sold a million copies of *Jubilee.* It was a best seller in France where they admitted printing 100,000 copies at a time. So *Jubilee* has seemed to make a fortune. I didn't get to be a millionaire by any means, but the royalty checks were wonderful Christmas presents. The Richard Wright book has not made a lot of money because of controversy around it, but I had already secured in advances and grants at least a hundred thousand dollars so I did not worry about how well it sold. Now that it is coming out in paperback, I feel that it will make some money.

The commercial value is not to be compared to the literary value of at least three of my books. *For My People* has stood out through these fifty years as a fine example of a black woman's poetry, and *Jubilee* has gone around the world and I never hear anything from people except that they liked that book and couldn't put it down until they finished it. The Richard Wright book has had remarkable coverage, not all of it positive, but not all of it negative, and it has gone through two precedent-shattering court cases, which make it a book that cannot be forgotten. The commercial value of my books has never been as great as the literary value. My books have been popular—that is, they have been successful with the people—and that is all I could wish.

That is a crowning statement for a career. What do you envision as an epilogue, so to speak?

I have had ill health all my life. They told my mother I would never live to be an adult. And my husband used to tease me and say, "Look how old you are. You weren't supposed to get to be thirty-five." Everything under the sun has happened to me, but I always have been optimistic. I really think I have had divine guidance and providential support because people tease me now and say, "Margaret doesn't have nine lives—she has twelve!" I'm like the cat with the nine lives. I have had five surgical operations, five pregnancies, and a stroke, but I am very optimistic about the future and I don't think I am going to die until my work is done.

Peter. East Baltimore, Maryland, 1969.

Left to right: Amina Dickerson, Jamila Thompson,
Julee Dickerson Thompson. Washington, DC, 1991.

C.L.R. James at the funeral of Dr. Leon Damas,
Rankin Chapel, Howard University.
Washington, DC, 1978.

Kai-Lynne Warren. St. Helena Island,
South Carolina, 1987.

Left to right: Ruby Quick, Wilford Streeter,
and Claudie Mae Bright. In the sand hills, near
Bennettsville, South Carolina, 1979.

Community elder, Willie ''Ashcan'' Jones.
Philadelphia, Pennsylvania, 1989.

Young family. St. Simon's Island, Georgia, 1977.

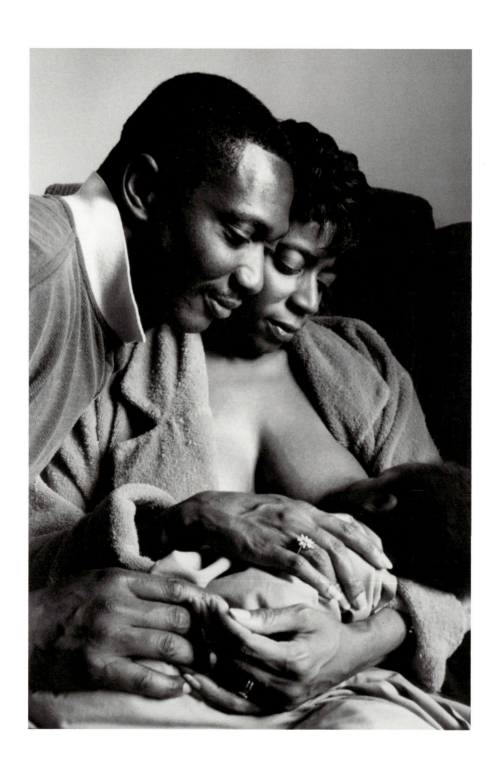

John and Lydia Horhn and their baby Charla Jade.
Jackson, Mississippi, 1992.

Mattie Lee Williams washing clothes.
Americus, Georgia, 1971.

The Davis family: Rita and Maceo, Sr.,
with their children, Paige and Maceo, Jr.
Philadelphia, Pennsylvania, 1989.

Sunday dinner at the home of Barbara and
Sinclair Whiteman, with their children and
grandchildren. North Philadelphia, 1988.

Thanking mom at commencement,
Howard University. Washington, DC, 1975.

Verta Mar teaching reading, Martin Behrman Middle
School. Algiers, New Orleans, Louisiana, 1985.

Arthur ''Pops'' Simpson's Jazz Alley:
A Sunday afternoon happening off East 50th Street,
Chicago, Illinois, 1976.

Saturday night at Cabana West, a neighborhood
bar in West Baltimore, Maryland, 1979.

Young people from the mule train
enjoying children's game, "Rise Sally Rise."
Duck Hill, Mississippi, 1968.

Sunday afternoon drumming in Druid Hill Park.
Baltimore, Maryland, 1973.

Fiddler Howard Armstrong entertaining guests at
the annual artists party in the home of Carl Owens.
Detroit, Michigan, 1986.

Gandy dancers (railroad workers). Mississippi, 1976.

Farmers. Americus, Georgia, 1971.

Mule train leaving Marks, Mississippi, for the
Washington, DC, Poor Peoples Campaign, 1968.

Homeless men around fire in front of
a shanty, N. 11th and Melon Streets,
Philadelphia, Pennsylvania, 1988.

Shopping on Gay Street.
East Baltimore, Maryland, 1973.

Holland Market. Baltimore, Maryland, 1978.

Muhammed Speaks newspaper salesmen
line up for inspection. Washington, DC, 1973.

Under arrest. Washington, DC (Anacostia), 1970.

Evening tent revival meeting.
Greenville, Mississippi, 1979.

James Baldwin at Peoples Congregational Church.
Washington, DC, 1979.

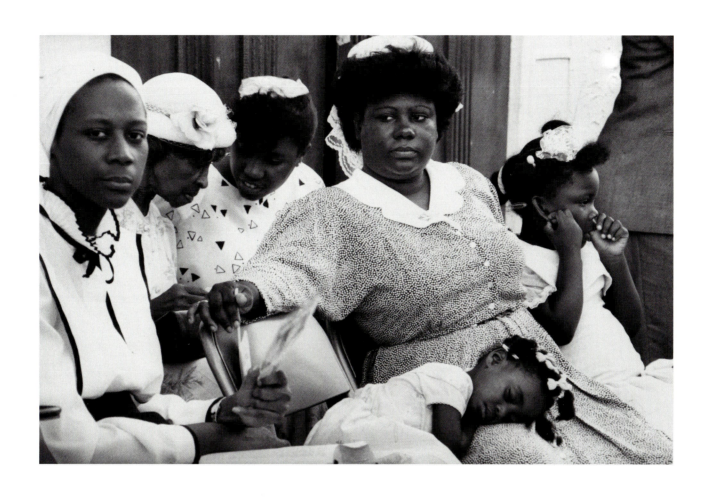

Sidewalk congregation of the Holy Church of the
Living God. West Philadelphia, Pennsylvania, 1989.

Muslim wedding. Baltimore, Maryland, 1985.

The family that prays together may stay together:
Smiley and Sylvia Fletcher gather their
children daily for afternoon prayer.
Philadelphia, Pennsylvania, 1988.

The Early's: James and Miriam and their sons
Ja-Ben and Jah-Mir. Washington, DC, 1982.

George and Beatrice Gosa relaxing on their
couch under quilts. Eutaw, Alabama, 1986.

Funeral. Fayette, Mississippi, 1976.

Meditating: 100-year-old quilter, Anner Brinner.
Port Gibson, Mississippi, 1992.

A TRIBUTE

This photo essay is my tribute to the rich cultural depths of Margaret Walker's classic poetry collection, *For My People,* and explores the impact of her poetry upon me. Each of the photographs seeks to capture the spirit of the people about whom Margaret Walker sings.

I selected photographs that call to mind the special human elements evoked by Walker, so basic to everyday life, and yet not often celebrated, elements which unveil the real beauty and the tenacity for life of African American people. These photographs are meant to complement the tones, movements, colors, and ethos of the poems in *For My People* while countering the distorted perspectives of African American communities presented on television and in print. For too many people images of drug-infested inner city ghettoes and bullet-riddled black bodies spewed across the urban landscape, are all they know about African Americans. Ignored are the millions of people in these same communities who are religious and hardworking, who love and care for their families and society, and whose lives are built upon a rich legacy of traditional culture.

Walker's lines are illuminating, provocative, and reverential, and I have tried to select photographs with those same qualities, regardless of their specific content relationship to any of the individual poems. In all the photographs, Walker's imagery and narratives have been interpreted through the photographic odyssey of my career.

It has been more than two decades since I first met Margaret Walker Alexander in Mississippi. She and her poetry taught me much about having my work reach down to capture my feelings, and about keeping the cultural flame lit and transmitting it to a future generation. I believe her poetic voice here is complemented by my photographs which, for me, speak visual poems about my people. My photographic vision is guided by the voices of the people in them, and, most of all, by the continuously heard voice of Walker.

This is a very personal essay that I share from my heart. The photographs are full of the light and darkness, the warmth and solitude that our people share, that all people share. With gratitude to Margaret, I offer this essay as a libation to the ancestors who have guided us both.

Roland L. Freeman